SIR EDMUND HILLARY'S

·SAGARMATHA·

Ed Hillary

Produced by **Hans Höfer** and **Lisa Choegyal**
Edited by **Lisa Choegyal** and **Wendy Brewer Lama**
Designed by **V. Barl**

INSIGHT TOPICS

Sir Edmund Hillary's

SAGARMATHA

Thyangboche Monastery beneath Ama Dablam.

Over one billion people revere the Himalaya and believe the mountains to be the abode or the embodiment of their gods.

Photograph by William Thompson

Everest is flanked by Lhotse (8,516 metres, 27,940 feet) and Nuptse (7,879 metres, 25,850 feet), with Makalu (8,463 metres, 27,766 feet) on the extreme right. Nepal has eight of the world's fourteen 8,000 metre (26,250 feet) mountains and eight of the ten highest mountains on earth.

Photograph by William Thompson

Mount Everest (8,848 metres, 29,028 feet) is the highest mountain in the world and rises as a rocky granite pyramid above surrounding Himalayan giants. Known as Sagarmatha (Mother of the Universe) in Nepal and Chomolungma (Mother Goddess) in Tibet, it is impressive in any language.

Photograph by William Thompson

The summit of Everest was first reached on 29 May 1953 by New Zealander Edmund Hillary and Tenzing Norgay Sherpa, who climbed by the South Col route (centre) above the perilous Khumbu Icefall.

Photograph by William Thompson

Although Mount Everest is by no means the most difficult peak in the Nepal Himalaya, it is the highest, most famous and attracts the greatest number of climbers. Ascents must be well planned and speedy as the body deteriorates dramatically above 8,000 metres (26,250 feet).

Photograph by William Thompson

Massive glaciers and icefalls cascade from both the Nepal and Tibet sides of Mount Everest. Seldom is the continuity of the massive scenery as from this unique Lear Jet eye-view.

Photograph by William Thompson

Dear Reader,

For all of us as climbers, trekkers or photographers, our image of Mount Everest is indelibly coloured by the Sherpa people who live in the high Khumbu Valley in the lap of Sagarmatha. Their over-flowing hospitality, wondrous monasteries and perpetual good nature enrich the experience of thousands of visitors who every year enjoy the Everest region. Without the Sherpas, the magnificent mountain world would be cold indeed.

From my first encounter with the Sherpas in 1951, I developed a commanding respect for these people who lived so cheerfully in such formidable surroundings. My warm affection broadened to concern over their health and livelihood as I realised the short-comings in their vulnerable existence.

With some mountaineering friends, I set up the Himalayan Trust in the early 1960s to finance and assist in environmental and welfare projects for the Sherpas. To help with fund-raising, we now have sister foundations in the USA, Canada and the UK. Today we provide education, medical and health care to hundreds of Sherpas through the construction of schools, hospitals, medical clinics, freshwater pipelines, reafforestation and bridge building projects.

This work has occupied much of my time for the last 30 years. I travel the world raising money and every year visit my Sherpa friends in Khumbu to monitor progress and see what else needs to be done. By now, they have taken over most of the legwork but I still enjoy sharing a glass of *chhang* in their homes and discussing ideas for new projects.

Just as our Khumbu projects seemed to be going smoothly, fate dealt us a heavy blow. On 19 January 1989, a fire destroyed the magnificent Thyangboche Monastery. Shock and sorrow reverberated throughout the Sherpa community and across continents to the thousands who had visited this revered site. We vowed to help rebuild this focal point of Sherpa heritage and culture and monument of historical significance.

Sagarmatha supports the Himalayan Trust by contributing funds to help with the rebuilding of the monastery, and in the future by giving financial assistance to the Trust's on-going work. This is its first official fund-raising book, made possible by the generous donation of all the photographs by my friends, many of them well-known people who have been linked with Everest over the years. Each image speaks a personal message; the result, superbly directed by Hans Höfer, is a masterpiece illustrating the life and beauty of Sagarmatha National Park in all its moods.

My thanks go to Hans Höfer for dreaming up this concept and for assisting the Himalayan Trust and the Sherpa people, as well as for providing all of us with beautiful images of a land and people we love.

Sir Edmund Hillary
Himalayan Trust
PO Box 224
Kathmandu, Nepal

◆ Ŝᴀɢᴀʀᴍᴀᴛʜᴀ ◆

John Tyson

On my travels around the world, at speaking engagements and fund raising functions for the Sherpas of the Everest region, I am often asked *"Why the Sherpas?"*. Why this book to benefit a relatively small population of mountain people among a wide world of need?

I answer that the Sherpas have something unique, worth protecting and nurturing not only for their future generations but for all of humanity — a culture and religion intertwined, which preserve a wealth of art, dance, rituals, scripts, customs and an unwavering set of altruistic morals that deserve a place in this world. They are blessed with the presence of Sagarmatha, the Nepalese name for the highest mountain on earth, meaning "Mother of the Universe", and a host of other reigning peaks. Ageless glaciers flowing from these giants feed the great rivers draining into the Ganges. The geologically young Himalayan range harbours some phenomenal plant, animal, bird and insect life. It is not heaven on earth,

An old Sherpa whirls his prayer wheel.

but to the some four thousand Sherpas who live there, and to the nearly ten thousand hikers who visit it each year, the Himalayan range is a remarkable and very special place.

Something in all of us wants to believe in a Shangrila. There is a universal appeal of a mythical Himalayan refuge of fertile valleys surrounded by thick forests and high mountains, where the people are happy and protected from strife. Being a Himalayan kingdom of reputed mystique, Nepal was once perceived as such a sanctuary. In fact few foreigners, save a handful of intrepid explorers, had at that time set foot in the country to verify the truth of this.

Indeed when I first visited Nepal in 1951 the country appeared, superficially at least, close to ideal. There were lush forests and carpets of wild flowers fringed with hardy junipers on the higher slopes and the people were warm, generous and cheerful. Most of my time was spent among the Khumbu Sherpas who, despite the cold and rigours of the high altitude, seemed in many ways to have a very good life.

John Hunt

Tenzing had been on Everest with foreign expeditions six times before his historic ascent of 1953. Here he is acclimatising and making the first ascent of Chhukung Peak with John Hunt, George Lowe and Alfred Gregory.

Ironically, what we outsiders observed as a harmonious existence was not far from the first Sherpas' reason for settling in Khumbu. The "people from the east" (the word *sher* means east, and *pa* people in Tibetan) migrated over the Nangpa La pass about 500 years ago, seeking what ancient Tibetan Buddhist texts described as a *beyul*, a sacred hidden valley concealed amidst the Himalaya. These *beyuls* were supposedly created by Padmasambhava, the sage who first introduced Buddhism to Tibet in the 8th century, who designed them as places of refuge for Tibetans in times of need.

The Sherpas prospered in the prolific Khumbu environment as farmers, herders and trans-Himalayan traders, with adequate resources for their limited needs. Pine, fir, rhododendron and birch trees

John Hunt

John Hunt took this picture of Makalu (8,463 metres, 27,766 feet) on 26 May 1953 from the couloir above the South Col of Everest.

provided all the wood they needed for building modest homes and splendid monasteries, for cooking and heating in a cold climate, fodder and bedding for their livestock quarters and shelter for wildlife. Even the fabled Yeti legend was carried over the Himalaya. Each family had adequate food, plus enough to feed the monks and lamas and stage dramatic seasonal festivals where fermented *chhang*, meat and delicacies were enjoyed. As traders they acquired enough wealth to generously adorn the monasteries with gold and exquisite artworks. The Sherpas evolved a spiritually wholesome although physically challenging existence among the highest mountains on earth, which they revered as the thrones of their gods.

Three "Everesters" from three nations meet at Namche Bazaar in 1963: James (Big Jim) Whittaker, Edmund Hillary and Norman Dyhrenfurth.

Natural barriers — the Himalaya on the north, east and west, nowhere lower than 5,700 metres (18,700 feet) and the Dudh Kosi River's narrow gorge on the south — kept the Khumbu sequestered from the outside world until the mid-20th century when Nepal first opened to visitors.

Then in 1950, the Sherpas' isolation was interrupted when the first foreign mountaineers arrived. Oscar Houston, his son Charles and Bill Tilman entered the Khumbu in search of a route up Mount Everest, which until then had only been accessible from the north side. Their expedition was very interesting but not really successful as they did not get far enough up the Khumbu glacier and came away convinced that access to Mount Everest from the south was not feasible at all.

The following year the British Mount Everest Reconnaissance Expedition, led by the redoubtable Eric Shipton, pushed much further up to the foot of the mountain. Eric and I climbed up 5,800 metres (19,000 feet) to a ridge of Pumori and were able to look up the Khumbu Icefall and into the Western Cwm. For the first time we realised that a potential route existed from the south and we even reached the crest of the formidable icefall.

The visitors' book at Pangboche monastery records the 1966 visit of the unlucky Unsoeld family whose father and daughter both died in mountaineering ventures.

It had been nearly 100 years since "Peak XV" had been identified as the highest in the world, interpreted from long-distance bearings and triangulation by the Survey of India. The first recorded height of 8,840 metres (29,002 feet) was later revised with improved measuring techniques to 8,848 metres (29,028 feet).

The British tried to find the great mountain's name, but when unsuccessful named it after Sir George Everest, Surveyor-General of India. Everest did in fact have a local name: Chomolungma to the Tibetans, and Sagarmatha to the Nepalese, both translated variously as "Mother Goddess". Straddling the border between Tibet and Nepal — obviously dominant when viewed from the north but not as impressive from the south — the mountain's supremacy had been recognised by indigenous inhabitants long before it was "discovered" by modern measurements.

The first attempt to scale Everest was made by British climbers from the Tibetan side in 1921, when Nepal was still closed to outsiders. George Leigh Mallory was the inspiration of the route finding and his name became synonymous with the mountain. In 1924 George Leigh Mallory and Andrew Irvine disappeared into the clouds around 8,200 metres (27,000 feet), leaving the world to wonder to this day whether or not they made it to the top. During the 1930s several other British attempts followed, but they were all unsuccessful although a number of climbers reached well over 8,000 metres (26,250 feet).

The 1978 yeti tracks photographed by John Hunt (now Lord John Hunt) in the Chola Khola.

The Swiss made two powerful bids for the summit of Everest in 1952 when Raymond Lambert and Tenzing Norgay Sherpa reached the 8,500 metre (27,890 feet) mark. Tenzing had been on the mountain with six expeditions, undertaking tasks ranging from high-altitude porter in his early days to being a member of the climbing team with the Swiss. Finally on 29 May 1953 Tenzing Norgay Sherpa and I battled through to the summit via the Southeast Ridge and both of us and Nepal were immediately catapulted into the international limelight.

The challenge of Mount Everest does not diminish over the years, and mountaineers seem to thrive on "firsts". In 1963, two Americans, Willi Unsoeld and Tom Hornbein, were the first climbers in the world to ascend and descend by different routes. In 1965, Nawang Gombu Sherpa of India became the first person to scale Everest twice, in 1963 and 1965. Yuichiro Miura of Japan was the first to descend a large part of Everest on skis in 1970, and five years later another Japanese, Mrs Junko Tabei, became the first woman to reach the summit of Everest.

Sherpa Tenzing Norgay (left) and Sir Edmund Hillary join the Rinpoche, or abbot, of Thyangboche Monastery.

All of the early expeditions on Everest used artificial oxygen, lugged up in heavy metal canisters. It was not until 1978 that Reinhold Messner of Italy and Peter Habeler of Austria first scaled Everest without the use of artificial oxygen, a feat previously considered physiologically impossible. A climb in the gruelling winter season was the next landmark when in 1980 Leszek Cichy and Krzysztof Wielicki of Poland made a February ascent, the same year that Reinhold Messner became the first individual to solo climb Everest, from the Tibet side. In 1988, Frenchman Marc Batard set an ascent speed record of 22.5 hours on a route already made by others, and in 1990 Ang Rita Sherpa of Nepal became the first person to scale Everest six times. My son Peter Hillary became the first son of a summiter to reach the top, in 1990 when he followed in my footsteps and ascended via our original route up the Southeast Ridge.

While the mountaineering world was engrossed in achievements, lands north of the Himalaya were in turmoil. In 1959 and into the early 1960s, a second migration of Tibetans fleeing Chinese occupation in Tibet were again in dire need of a *beyul*. The Sherpas, whose religion rewards generosity and honours hospitality, were obliged to take them in. With the closure of the Tibet border to trade, the Sherpas' lucrative role as trans-Himalayan traders and middlemen in the exchange of highland and lowland products ceased, depriving them of vital sources of income.

The balance which for generations the Sherpas had maintained with nature was upset by the influx of Tibetan refugees with their herds of grazing animals. The demands of a growing number of foreign mountaineering expeditions included wood for cooking fuel and the introduction of the concept of a cash economy. The forests that had been carefully managed by community guards, who levied penalties for cutting green wood and permitted felling of saplings only for religious needs, were slashed by the Sherpas themselves who found an easy market for firewood.

Each expedition would use an estimated 120 kilograms of firewood a day, amounting to 7,200 kilograms or more over two to three months, multiplied by the number of expeditions. At this rate, it did not take long for the slopes above Namche to be stripped bare, and nearly every hillside within an hour's walk to be alarmingly thinned. With deforestation came severe erosion, washing valuable topsoil downstream forever. Without forests to produce the means for continued regeneration, and with rampant over-grazing by goats introduced to augment the meat supply, new tree seedlings did not have a chance.

Those Sherpas who were involved in the tourism trade prospered and could afford the escalating food and commodity prices which the foreign invasion had induced; but others suffered the inflationary effects and were driven either to sign up for hazardous mountaineering work or to cut more wood.

The echoing growls of the monks' long horns reverberate across valleys and haunt the soul.

Tragedy struck many a home in Khumbu, whether from climbing accident or family dissolution brought on by the men's long absences from home. In the old days, the practice of polyandry had assured the Sherpanis, women Sherpas, of at least one resident husband at any time, while his brother or brothers were away on trading trips. But as ideas from the outside world infiltrated, monogamous relationships had begun to take hold and the women were left alone to tend the crops, children and community needs. Some Sherpanis carried porter loads but none aspired to climb.

The world rallies to support the rebuilding of Thyangboche Monastery, razed by fire on 19 January 1989.

What was happening to the Sherpas' Shangrila?

Those of us who had been enchanted by their mountain paradise began to worry about Khumbu's future. Would the shift toward a wage-earner economy disrupt the social system and undermine the religious values and rituals which the Sherpas had preserved from their Tibetan heritage? Without forests, what would become of the wildlife — the elusive snow leopard, the shaggy Himalayan tahr, the oddly-fanged musk deer, the shy marmot, the Himalayan hare, the brilliant Impeyan pheasant and soaring griffon? What was the future for these glacier-sculpted valleys whose rock once lay beneath the primordial Tethys Sea, were then uplifted and turned on end some 40 to 60 million years ago?

I had spent quite a bit of time with the Sherpas over the years and increasingly I had become aware of the things they lacked in their rugged existence: primarily, schools for their children and medical treatment for their sick.

By 1961, I had decided to do something about it. I raised the necessary funds and we constructed the Khumjung school, the first permanent school in the area. Thus the Himalayan Trust was established as a body to raise money and to plan and supervise a growing number of projects. From every corner of Khumbu, Pharak and Solu, the three Sherpa regions, petitions poured in for schools, hospitals, medical clinics, bridges and drinking water pipelines. The Trust never initiated a project but was ready to respond to a community's requests with funds and technical advice where needed. Sherpas of all ages contributed their labours and materials, often working alongside my family and friends. Communities were responsible for maintaining their projects.

Attempting to unravel the mysteries of the video age.

As more parents wanted to educate their children, the Khumjung school was expanded, later with a hostel so that older students from further villages could attend and live there during the week. It was heartening to see the first graduating class of boys and girls from Khumjung school and to speculate on the difference education would make in their lives.

To help in the transport of building materials, the Trust constructed an airfield at Lukla. It saved time and money in accomplishing our projects, but also had the unplanned side-effect of giving tourists much easier access to the Everest area.

The newly formed trekking industry provided a more amenable occupation to many Sherpas, and to their wives and families. It was not dangerous and was more seasonal, allowing the men to be home during winter and summer months. It came at exactly the right moment. His Majesty's Government of Nepal had banned all foreign mountaineering expeditions from spring 1966 until 1969, thereby removing a major Sherpa source of income.

Nepal's first trekkers, three middle-aged American women, hiked into Khumbu in spring 1965 escorted by Lt Col Jimmy Roberts, the founder of Mountain Travel and a veteran of many Nepal expeditions and first ascents. Nepal's trekking industry was born. Mountain Travel Nepal is still one of the kingdom's leading trekking agencies to this day. With its spectacular scenery and relatively quick access via the Lukla airfield, Khumbu was an instant success; and the Sherpas proved naturally adept at trek guiding. Many have gone on to establish their own trekking agencies and through their contact with foreigners, many Sherpa children now receive education sponsorships both in Nepal and abroad.

New arrivals at Lukla airfield.

We eventually came to realise that some sort of control over tourism was needed to prevent Khumbu from becoming a treeless high-altitude desert. Nepal had nationalized the country's forests and shifted more political control to the central government, further undermining the Sherpas' protectiveness toward their natural resources. Yet it was difficult to rely on the central government administration to look after such a remote mountain region.

In 1976, after a number of studies and discussions, the Everest region was designated as a national park. His Majesty's Government of Nepal asked the New Zealand government to help in establishing the Sagarmatha National Park. For the first six years, New Zealanders provided park wardens and rangers to advise and develop a management plan. Several Sherpa graduates of the Khumjung school were sent to New Zealand for training in park and resource management and later served as the park's warden.

To us a national park seemed like the only solution, but to the Sherpas, who were suddenly saddled with strict regulations governing wood cutting and grazing, the national park was the enemy. They feared that, as had been done in some of Nepal's earlier national parks, the human population would be resettled and their homeland would be reserved for the trees, animals and tourists.

The Impeyan pheasant is the national bird of Nepal, where it is also known as the danphe (bird of nine colours).

The Sherpas' fears over relocation proved unfounded. The park initiators, and subsequently UNESCO in declaring Sagarmatha National Park a World Heritage Site, had recognised the cultural importance of the Sherpas as well as the significance of the world's highest mountains and its associated flora and fauna. It remains one of the few national parks in the world where the indigenous people are integral to the preservation of the total environment; village lands are excluded from the national park boundaries.

High altitude photographs are essential tools in the difficult task of accurately mapping the Everest region.

One of the wardens' greatest challenges has been to gain the support of the people and to convince them that the park regulations are in their long-term interests. To do so, the park joined in making improvements for the Sherpas' and visitors' mutual benefits. A visitor centre with interpretive displays, three trekker lodges providing a model for private facilities, bridges and other projects were constructed. His Majesty's Government and UNESCO jointly financed a mini-hydro electric facility below Namche. Other alternative energy schemes, such as solar chargers and more efficient stoves, have become popular.

Park regulations now require all trekking groups and expeditions to be self-sufficient in kerosene for cooking, although most porters still rely on firewood as do independent trekkers who stay in local lodges. When the ground-stripping eating habits of the goats grew to devastating proportions, every goat in Khumbu was rounded up and the Himalayan Trust paid their owners a fair price and ushered them out of the region forever.

Litter has become a major problem of mounting international concern, along the trail, at expedition base camps and high camps. In such a cold climate, rubbish takes years to disintegrate and non-biodegradable products pile up indefinitely. Some innovative farmers and lodge keepers have built composting toilets where they add livestock manure and dried pine needles to make a rich fertiliser for their crops.

There is much visitors can do to minimise their impact on the natural and cultural environment of Khumbu. Not to litter or pollute should be obvious, especially around sacred

Living in the Himalayan range has its advantages, not least of which is the view.

areas. Be prepared for cold weather with appropriately warm clothes so as not to rely on wood heating, and preclude emergencies which unnecessarily risk Sherpa staff's safety. Trekkers should choose a responsible trekking agency which upholds conservation standards. If staying in local lodges, cut down on firewood use by ordering food at the same time as others. Visitors who respect the local customs and beliefs with sensitive behaviour, and do not contribute to inflation by paying exorbitantly, will be doubly rewarded with genuine hospitality and the knowledge that they have left behind a good impression of their country.

Tourism's far-reaching potential to bring the world closer together, to know first-hand the ways of life and attitudes of another culture, is nowhere easier realised than in Khumbu. But if the natural environment continues to suffer, perhaps the only solution lies in closing the national park to allow the plant and animal life to recuperate. Unfortunately, this solution would hurt the Sherpas who have become economically dependant on the tourist business.

The Himalayan Trust continues to be active, widening its reach and broadening its programmes. We have tried to re-establish the denuded forests by setting up tree nurseries. Sherpas have planted a million seedlings, using only native species, but the trees grow very slowly at high altitudes and many do not survive due to the cold, birds, deer and yaks. Electric fencing protects the planted areas, run on a solar charged battery. The yaks — and the curious Sherpa kids — got the shock of their lives the first time they touched a wire.

One of the greatest misfortunes of the Sherpas' recent history was the loss of Thyangboche monastery. On 19 January 1989 a fire blazed through the 77-year old religious centrepiece of Khumbu, destroying the entire structure along with ancient scripts, books, frescoes and its ritually significant trappings. It was the sanctuary of 36 monks and 25 students, headed by the revered incarnate lama, the Rinpoche Nawang Tenzing Zangpo. They have carried on the study of Mahayana Buddhism in the Tibetan tradition since the founding of the first monastery in Khumbu some 350 years ago.

Thousands of trekkers know Thyangboche as the site of the autumn Mani Rimdu dance festival where the monks don silk robes and vibrant masks and become their gods. The drama celebrates the victory of good over evil, of Buddhism over the Bon religion and invokes blessings for the coming year.

Thyangboche monastery will stand again. From the first murmuring about reconstruction among the Rinpoche and people of Khumbu, I promised the Sherpas that the Himalayan Trust would assist in replacing the focal point of their heritage and culture — one of the world's most sacred historical monuments. The Sherpa community generously contributed cash and labour and other international donors lent their support. Years of labour go into building such an architectural masterpiece, from the intricate carving of wood beams to the extensive, elaborate wall paintings depicting gods and spirits of the Buddhist pantheon. The new Thyangboche monastery is designed to be an enlarged and improved replica of its former self.

Although it has suffered the ravages of time, the Everest region is still a magnificent place to visit, and deservedly one of Nepal's most renowned visitor destinations. The valley leading up to the southern face of Sagarmatha is a spectacular walk, dotted with Sherpa stone-house villages, and on every side world-famous peaks jut into the azure sky. Few high-altitude hiking areas in the world are so accessible, offer such breathtaking camping sites and comfortable tourist lodges. The quiet valleys of Thame, Gokyo and Dingboche have maintained their traditional lifestyles, their inhabitants are still reliant on agriculture and livestock herding. Through all the changes, the Sherpas have held fast to their deep-rooted traditions, valuing compassion for others and an unshakable faith in their deities.

That is my answer to the question "Why the Sherpas?" for those who have time to listen. It is my ambition to help them restore their lost Shangrila, not to deny them the advantages of modern technology but to allow them the breadth of understanding necessary to make the wisest choices. My contributions are finite but through the Himalayan Trust and the donations received from this book all of our dreams can come true and the Khumbu *beyul* of the early Tibetan scripts will live forever.

A wooden block-print of a lhu spirit, the goddess guardian of water sources and rain, Junbesi, 1965.

Since Nepal first opened in 1949, there have been successive assaults on Everest. No early mountaineering expeditions could have managed without the support of Sherpas, both men and women, and their yaks. Here the equipment for the 1975 British South West Face Expedition arrives at Base Camp.

Photograph by Hamish MacInnes

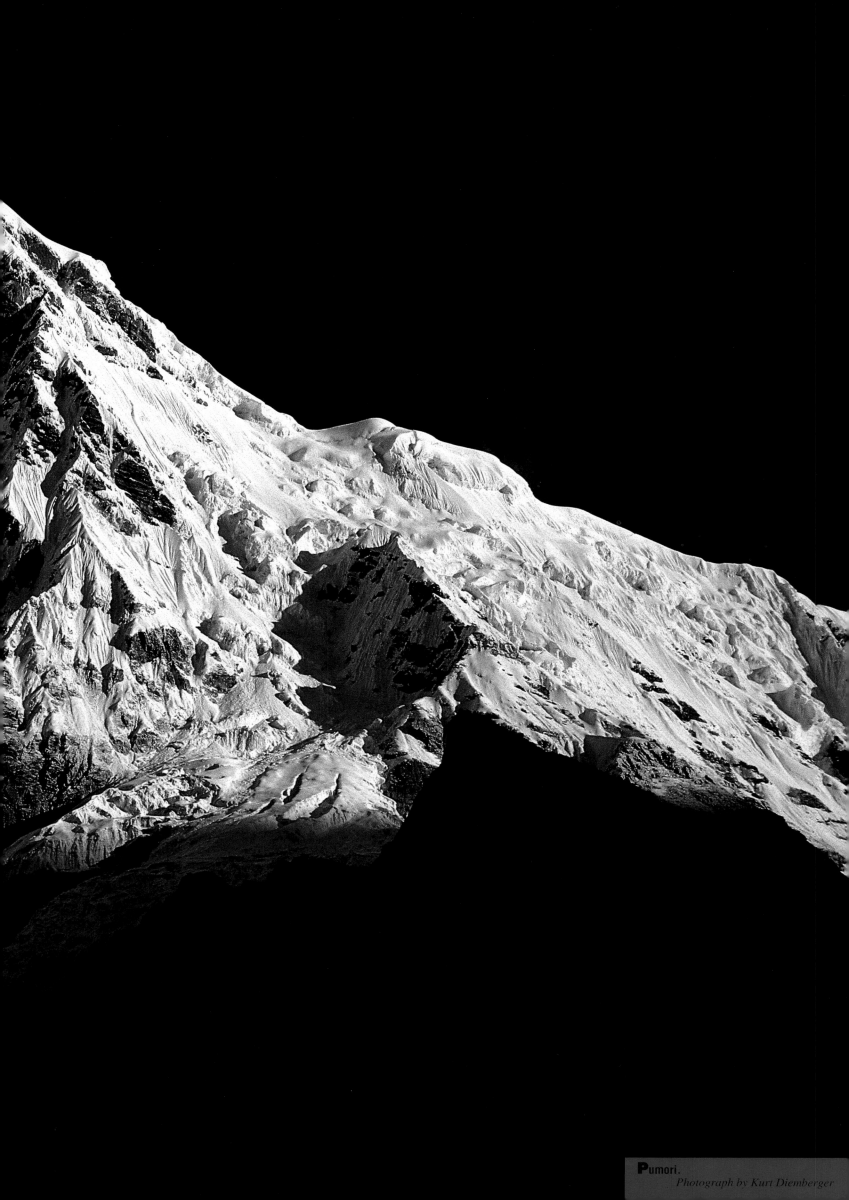

Pumori.
Photograph by Kurt Diemberger

The precipitous apex of Cholatse epitomises the magic and mystery which visitors hope for in the Himalaya. The hillside invites us to explore but what will we find?

Photograph by Dr David R Shlim

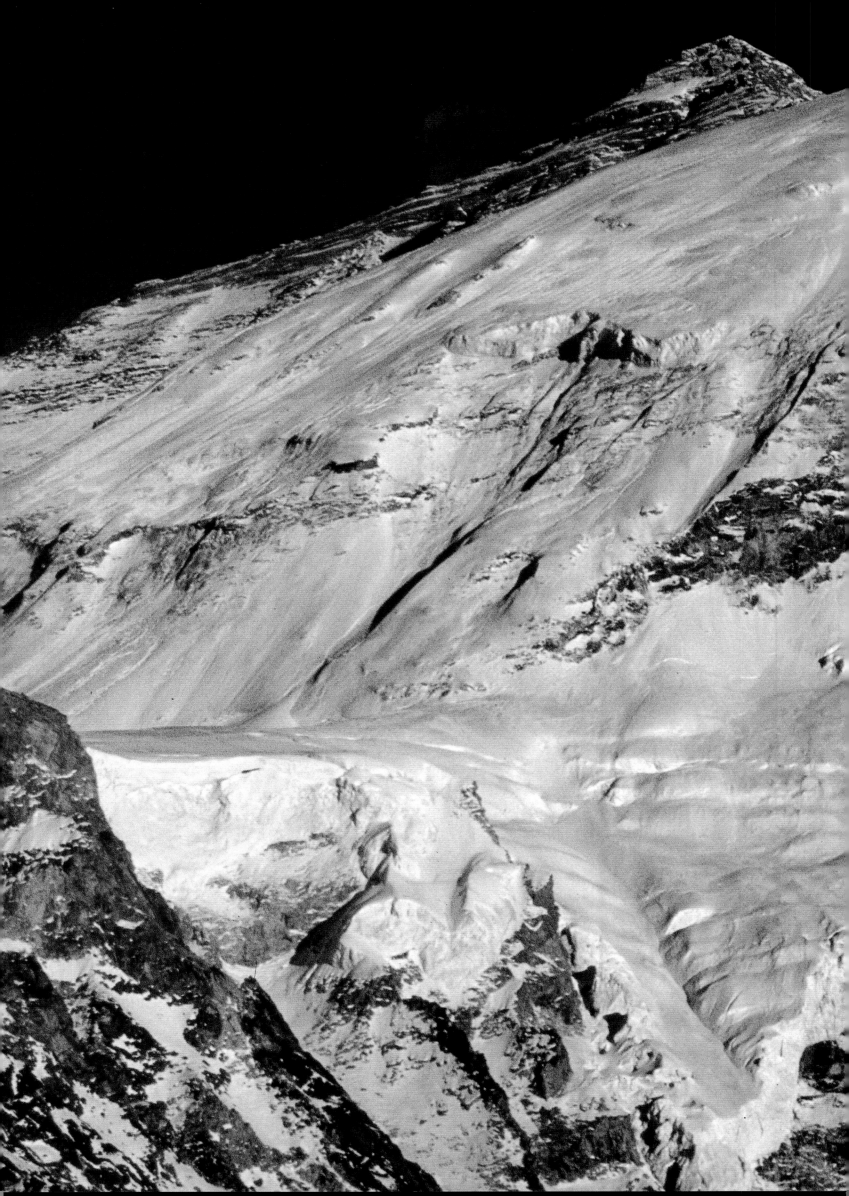

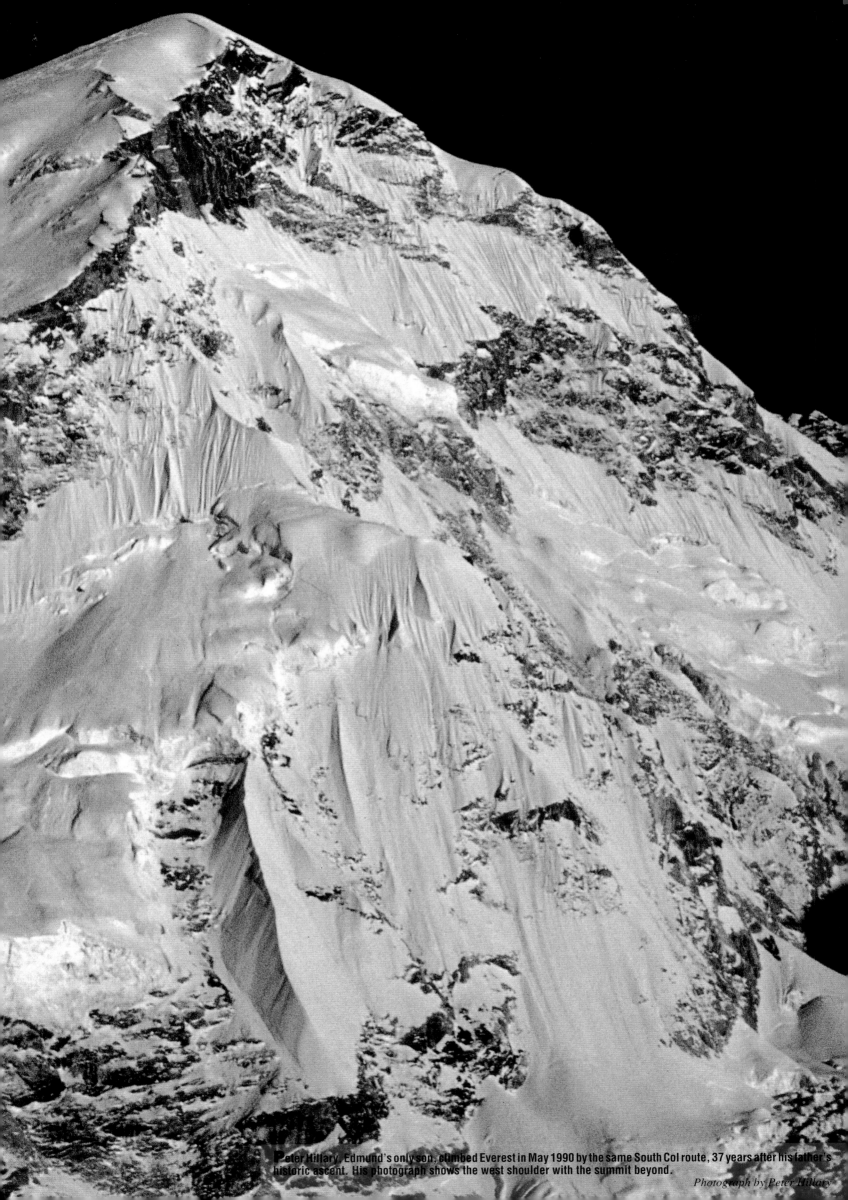

Peter Hillary, Edmund's only son, climbed Everest in May 1990 by the same South Col route, 37 years after his father's historic ascent. His photograph shows the west shoulder with the summit beyond.

Photograph by Peter Hillary

The imagination soars with the raven, whose bowed head takes in the expansive, grand scale of the Everest Base Camp region. In the mountains, a short moment captures our aspirations and lives on.

Photograph by Lawrence Shlim

A priceless moment caught as dinner is being prepared by this tiny lake beneath Tawoche; the sunset peaks reflect in the still water, the afternoon mist lingers and the moon is already risen.

Photograph by Dr David R Shlim

Misty morning at Thyangboche. After a winter spent in the ancient continent of Australia preparing his book, *The Songlines*, writer Bruce Chatwin passed an enchanted spring among the youngest mountain range.

Photograph by Bruce Chatwin

A classic view of Everest, Lhotse and Ama Dablam taken from a ridge above Khumjung on a 1973 trek marking the 20th anniversary of Everest's first ascent, by the expedition leader.

Photograph by John Hunt

The Himalayan tahr (*Himitragus jemlahicus*), gathered here near Phortse, are a wild goat. Even the youngest leap with amazing agility on the steep cliffs. Their numbers are increasing rapidly with the establishment of the national park.

Photograph by Robert and Linda Fleming

The Himalayan griffon (*Gyps himalayensis*) tries to launch from a cliff top perch. This heaviest flying bird in the Himalaya has a wingspan of some two and half metres (eight feet) and must rely on updrafts to gain altitude. Well over a hundred bird species, including the colorful danphe, national bird of Nepal, find food and shelter in Sagarmatha National Park.

Photograph by Robert and Linda Fleming

▲ Swallowtail butterfly (*Papilio machaon ssp*) is rare in England but not uncommonly found in the highlands of Nepal. This one was sunning itself at 3,000 metres (10,000 feet) near base camp, a wonderful encounter after six weeks amid snow and ice.

Photograph by Simon Brown

Himalayan flora extends far above that of other ranges: several species of dwarf juniper and rhododendron grow up to 5,000 metres (16,400 feet). Here, in May at 3,500 metres (11,500 feet) near Namche Bazaar, this spring flowering pea, *Thermopsis barbata*, shows a fuzzy whitish growth contrasting beautifully with the maroon flowers.

Photograph by Robert and Linda Fleming

Rhododendrons grow the length of Nepal but are more common in the eastern reaches of the country. The white species (*Rhododendron lindleyi*) has a marvellous fragrance and grows above Lukla at about 3,000 metres (10,000 feet)

Photograph by Robert and Linda Fleming

Mountain wildflowers cover the hillsides during monsoon: the walk between Namche and Thyangboche is celebrated as the "most beautiful in the world". This hauntingly lovely Himalayan blue poppy was photographed by Bonington on his way to Everest in 1972

Photograph by Chris Bonington

There are over 30 species of rhododendron found in Nepal, varying in size from huge trees to dwarf species only a few centimetres high. They are celebrated as the national flower, *laligurans*.

Photograph by Norman G Dyhrenfurth

Only once every few years, as in May 1980 when this picture was taken, do the *Rhododendron arboreum* below Thyangboche Monastery synchronise their flowering, enjoyed by the 50 or so resident monks on their frequent walks to Namche. The deep red blossom fades to pink and eventually white at the higher altitudes.

Photograph by Robert and Linda Fleming

"Every half mile or so we would pass a wall of stone slabs, each one carved with the mantra *Om Mani Padme Hum* (Hail the Jewel in the Lotus)." (Elizabeth Chatwin) *Mani* walls, and all sacred monuments, should be passed on the left to enable the prayers' release to the gods.

Photograph by Bruce Chatwin

Mani stone and prayer flag above the village of Dingboche illustrate the harmonious integration that these religious symbols have with the landscape. Chhukung glacier is on the distant right.

Photograph by Lawrence Shlim

Sunlight penetrates the afternoon cloud highlighting the village of Phortse. Off the main trading and trekking trails, Phortse remains unaffected by Western tourism; a visit is like stepping back in time.

Photograph by Bruce E Jefferies

Forests still surround the monsoon-rich fields of Phortse, carved out of the hillside. High above the village are the ruins of an old monastery.

Namche Bazaar is the Sherpa capital. Perched above the Dudh Kosi River, nestled in a bowl protected by the god-mountain Khumbila, it represents the very heart of the Khumbu.

Photograph by Hans Höfer

Namche Bazaar in the winter of 1975, memorable for its unusually heavy snowfall.
Photograph by Michael Dillon

Kunde village after a late snow storm as seen from the house of Mingma Tsering, Edmund Hillary's head sherpa and friend.

Photograph by Frances Klatzel

Monks' houses nestle below the red-washed walls of Thame Monastery looking west towards the Tashi Lapcha pass.
Photograph by Norman G Dyhrenfurth

Most of the old wood-shingle roofs of Namche Bazaar, held down against storms with rows of rocks, have been replaced since this picture was taken in 1973, many with corrugated iron. Traditional prayer flags still flutter in the wind.

Photograph by B Ned Kelly

Elegant carved window frames are typical of more affluent Sherpas' houses. This one belongs to the house of Kuso Dawa Tsering in Namche.

Photograph by Hans Höfer

Monastery doors constructed of massive wood are rare at such altitudes and must be carried considerable distances at great expense. *Tsampa* (barley flour) thumbprints are for protection, as are the wood block prints.

Photograph by Hans Höfer

The kitchen is the centre of the house where mud-blackened pots on the *chulo* (oven) await the family's return for the midday meal. Nearly every household in Khumbu uses a plastic expedition drum for storage these days.

Photograph by Mal Clarbrough

Traditional striped woven aprons are worn both back and front by Sherpanis, who still prefer their practical *chuba* dress to modern clothing.

Photograph by Hans Höfer

Kapa Temba, the painter son of Mingma Tsering, is deaf since birth. He was a pupil of the great Sherpa artist Kapa Kalden of Khumjung, whose work included the lost murals of Thyangboche as well as many village and home *gompas*.

Photograph by Peter Hillary

Developed from the Tibetan mural style of paintings, the Sherpa primitives depict with great charm the villages and monasteries of the upper Khumbu valley and are now very popular with visitors. This is one of the last painted by Kapa Kalden himself, the father of this adapted style.

Photograph by Bruce E Jefferies

The Saturday market is a feature of life in Namche Bazaar, bringing together traders from the lower elevations to bargain and barter with Sherpas from all over Khumbu.

Photograph by Lawrence Shline

Maize is carried for days from the lowlands where it is grown. The week's supply is measured and carried off in a makeshift sack.

Photograph by Mal Clarbrough

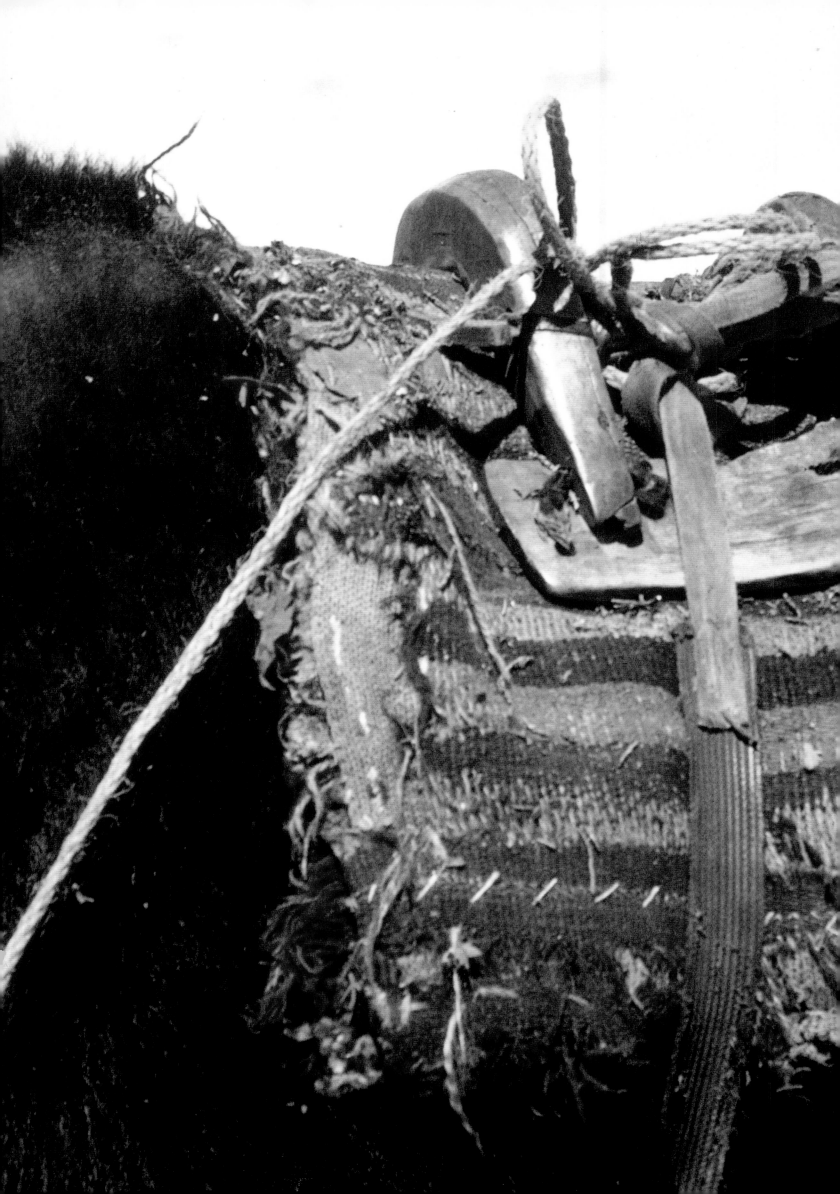

Yaks and *dzos* are essential to life at these altitudes providing milk, cheese, dung for fertiliser and burning, hair for weaving, leather and meat. They are also important beasts of burden, capable of carrying double the loads of a person, tied on to a simple saddle arrangement.

Photograph by Peter Hillary

The chill wind of winter blows at the weekly Namche Bazaar

Photograph by John Tyson

Sherpas are great meat-eaters, although their Tibetan Buddhist religion precludes them from killing animals themselves.

Photograph by Peter Hillary

The way of the world on the trail. Even marathon runner Richard Crane found a brief moment to pause and enjoy a moment in Khumbu with lowland porters on his record-breaking epic run the length of the Himalaya in 1983.

Photograph by Richard Crane

People of Phortse enjoy a joke in the sun whilst collecting firewood. The national park restricts the cutting of wood and encourages the use of kerosene.

Photograph by B Ned Kelly

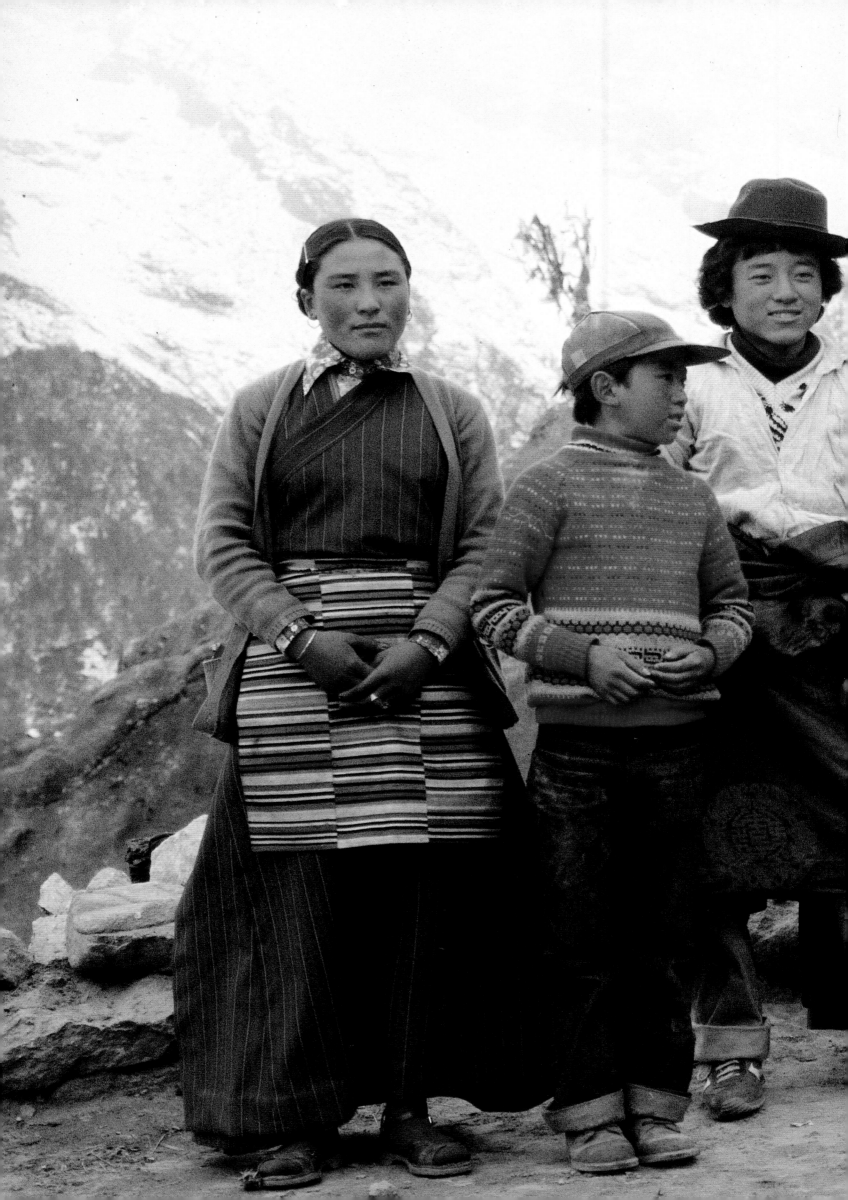

The family of Pasang Norbu line up, some reluctantly, above Namche in their best combination of traditional and modern clothes. Coral, turquoise and dzi stones, strung and worn as necklaces, are much prized by Sherpanis and are traded at incredible prices.

Photograph by Mal Clarbrough

In 1976, while this Sherpa woman spent her days tending animals and growing crops amidst the harsh environment of her simple stone-built home, her son was studying in New Zealand for a Bachelors Degree in Parks and Natural Resources Management. Her necklace, representing the family wealth, was donned especially for the photograph.

Photograph by Bruce E Jefferies

Sen Tenzing, a veteran guide well into his eighties in this 1982 portrait, holds his "tiger book" with entries dating from the 1930s expeditions. Sen Tenzing accompanied the very first party of Westerners into the Khumbu, including Charles Houston and Bill Tilman in 1950. Sen Tenzing was again with Eric Shipton and Edmund Hillary in 1951 when they first identified a feasible route up the mountain.

Photograph by Galen Rowell

Distinguished Sherpa elder, Konjo Chumbi and his wife, live in Khumjung and are regarded with great respect by the Sherpa community. Famous for his knowledge of old stories, songs and dances, he was chosen to safeguard the precious yeti relics on their 1963 tour to Chicago, New York and Paris. In London he presented the Queen and Prince Philip with Sherpa robes and hats.

Photograph by Frances Klatzel

The late Dawa Tenzing, veteran of Everest expeditions from Tibet as early as 1922 and 1924
Photograph by Mal Clarbrough

Although unable to remember the names of Mallory and Irvine, Dawa Tenzing did recall, during a pre-war expedition, two young *sahibs* setting off for the top of Everest, never to return.

Photograph by Leo Dickinson

It is a precarious life for young children in the smoke-filled stone Sherpa houses on steep hillsides. Carried tied onto their mothers back they are safe and nurtured.

Photograph by Hans Höfer

A yak near Phortse. Yaks are often bred with cows to produce the male *dzopkyo* (*dzo* for short) and the female *dzum*. The cross is considered less temperamental than the pure bred yaks. They can also tolerate lower elevations and the females produce more milk.

Photograph by Norman G Dyhrenfurth

Since 1983, there have been no goats in Khumbu, save for an occasional one brought up for slaughter. The Great Round-up was arranged by the Himalayan Trust to save the delicate flora. The Trust purchased all the goats, collected them together on the open spaces of the Syangboche airstrip and had them driven down-valley where grazing was plentiful.

Photograph by Michael Dillon

A farm worker protects newly sown seeds from the birds with foliage.
Photograph by John Hunt

A wide trail leads up through the thickly forested Dudh Kosi valley to Khumbu. Among the Blue Himalayan pine (*Pinus wallichiana*) and Silver fir (*Abies spectabilis*), the flaky red bark and of the Himalayan birch (*Betula utilis*) draped with *Usnea* lichen is perhaps most memorable.

Photograph by Hans Höfer

Pine needles are collected for animal bedding, carried here in a *doko* basket supported by a strap on the forehead. Mixed with manure, it will eventually become a rich fertiliser used on the fields.

Photograph by Hans Höfer

Photograph by Mal Clarbrough

Development comes to the Khumbu with much physical effort. Doors and pre-cut window frames are portered to the Lobuche lodge construction site from the national park workshop in Namche, several days away.

On a ridge high above the villages of Khumjung and Kunde is the memorial to Edmund Hillary's first wife and younger daughter, who were killed in an aircraft accident in Nepal in 1975. This spot overlooks the valley, with Ama Dablam on the left.

Photograph by Hans Höfer

"Sange said that every ... prayer ... straight to heaven.
Prayer flags everywhere ... to this country, and we felt
surrounded by blessings ...

Photograph by Bruce Chatwin

"The night dew had frozen on a string of prayer flags that seemed to disappear into an infinity of darkness. Why do we need prayer flags at base camp in the Himalaya and nowhere else?" (*David R Shlim, Baruntse Expedition 1980*)

Photograph by Dr David R Shlim

Unperturbed by the cold, shaggy yaks ruminate beneath a *chorten* in the monochromatic landscape of a bleak winter day. Buddhist *chortens*, containing holy relics, are found all over the Khumbu marking passes and sacred spots.

Photograph by Bruce E Jefferies

Near Namche the Sherpa festival of Dumji is celebrated annually in honour of Khumbila, the goddess of the Khumbu as embodied in the sacred mountain. The air is filled with fragrant juniper incense and participants are dressed in their best clothes.

Photograph by Mal Clarbrough

Not only their best clothes but also the best *chhang*, locally brewed beer, is kept specially for the summer Dumji festival. Offerings bode well for a productive growing season and harvest.

Photograph by Mal Clarbrough

Prayer flags are blessed and replaced, offerings made and the *mani* wall repainted during this monsoon festival.

Photograph by Bruce E Jefferies

Beneath rhododendrons, prayers are offered on an auspicious April day by the Thyangboche monks accompanied with drums and horns. The abbot of the monastery, the Thyangboche Rinpoche, leads the proceedings from his seat at the far end.

Photograph by Frances Klatzel

Sherpanis prepare to dance during the 1981 festivities at the site of the Sagarmatha National Park Visitor Centre at Mendelphu, above Namche, marking the end of New Zealand's six years of involvement in assisting Nepal in the development of Sagarmatha National Park.

Photograph by Mal Clarbrough

Thyangboche Monastery was swept away by fire only a few weeks after this picture was taken by Bradford Washburn and his wife Barbara. After presenting his National Geographic Everest map to the King of Nepal in Kathmandu, veteran scientist-adventurer Washburn was able to realise his dream with a one and three quarter hour visit to the monastery via helicopter.

Photograph by Bradford Washburn

This masked dancer portrays the god of compassion at the great Mani Rimdu festival at Thyangboche. One young monk, when asked how he could dance with only tiny holes in the mask's nostrils to see through replied, "We don't need to see. When we put on the masks, we become gods."

Photograph by Frances Klatzel

Three monks rehearse without costumes the day before the Mani Rimdu in November 1977 at Thyangboche in order to synchronise their steps with the music. Mani Rimdu is also celebrated at the *gompas* of neighbouring Thame and Chiwong in Solu.

Photograph by Mary Plage

Mani Rimdu lasts over several days and takes the form of a blessing ceremony wishing all present a long spiritual life, followed by the dance drama. The closing ceremony is a crescendo of music and drums.

Photograph by Frances Klatzel

The Guardian King of the West whirls back to back with the Guardian King of the East during a sequence in the Mani Rimdu dance drama at Thyangboche. The festival celebrates good over evil and the triumph of the Buddhist faith over early demons.

Photograph by Mary Plage

Spinning prayer wheels energises the Buddhist prayers written on long scrolls, ritually blessed and rolled within each.

Photograph by Frances Klatzel

Thyangboche during the Mani Rimdu festival. Every first-time visitor to a remote Tibetan Buddhist monastery must pause for a moment and wonder if the secrets of life and happiness are hidden inside. The power and mystery are captured in the atmosphere.

Photograph by Dr David R Shlim

A life dedicated to contemplation.
Photograph by Peter Hillary

Young monks are often supported in their studies by their families, who consider it an honour. Their study of religious books, made with wood-blocks printed on long loose-leaf pages, is relieved with salt butter tea served in bowls. These same monks mix meditation with childish joy whilst playing with a frisbee in their maroon robes.

Photograph by Galen Rowell

This remarkable 1953 image shows a Thyangboche monk block printing on the handmade paper then manufactured at the monastery.

Photograph by Hamish MacInnes

The elegant symmetry of Ama Dablam dominates the landscape and imprints the mind.
Photograph by Peter Hillary

Now destroyed by fire these Thyangboche murals depicting a popular religious story must be repainted

Photograph by Kurt Diemberger

A protector deity on the walls of Thyangboche monastery was photographed on the way to the south west face of Everest in 1972. All expeditions pause to offer prayers en route to the mountain.

Photograph by Chris Bonington

Every Buddhist monastery or *gompa* is built within a prescribed layout. Images of the gods and their stories are an important aid to meditation, and are a curiosity to the awe-struck visitor.

Photograph by Chris Bonington

The yeti scalp and hand from Pangboche Monastery are treasured artifacts, though they did not withstand scientific scrutiny by visiting specialists. The scalp is similar to the one in Khumjung that was displayed in the West by Edmund Hillary and Desmond Doig in 1963.

Photograph by Galen Rowell

Paranormal phenomena are accepted philosophically by the Sherpas of the Khumbu. This *torma*, a *tsampa* and butter effigy, was made for an old man who had died in Namche. The next day a fine brittle "hair" had magically grown all over it, believed by the family to belong to the dead man. David Shlim and his friend Brot Coburn took samples, which reminded them of a "delicate kind of tinsel", but the hair mysteriously disappeared before it could be analysed. All that remains is this photograph.

Photograph by Dr David R Shlim

Yetis live in the sub-conscious of all Sherpas, even if expeditions are unable to locate them or Western science prove their existence. This boy, a student of artist Kapa Kalden, was drawing beneath the peaks in Khumjung.

Photograph by Galen Rowell

A helicopter evacuated Woodrow Wilson Sayre in 1962 from Lukla after his unauthorised attempt on Everest from the north failed. Nowadays helicopters are not such a rare or confusing sight for Sherpa children as then.

Photograph by Norman G Dyhrenfurth

Sound recordings made in 1958 are listened to with fascination by Thyangboche *lamas* and novices. An expedition in search of the yeti, popularised as the Abominable Snowman, had been seeking audible evidence.

Photograph by Norman G Dyhrenfurth

Syangboche airstrip at 3,800 metres (12,500 feet) has to be laboriously cleared of snow by hand. This Swiss-made Pilatus Porter, straining on its brakes, brings in supplies and is a tenuous link with the outside world.

Photograph by Bruce E Jefferies

Leo Dickinson and his wife Mandy have yet to achieve flying in a hot-air balloon over Everest into Tibet but have dared push the limits in the high valleys. Here Dickinson, foreground, is taking off from Thyangboche. The Gokyo valley extends into the background.

Photograph by Leo Dickinson

Ama Dablam dominates the skyline. "An open balloon is a marvellous way of viewing the Himalaya – that is, until you land!" (Leo Dickinson)

Photograph by Mandy Dickinson

An ingenious cantilever bridge below Namche. Where high-tech fixes aren't available, the Sherpas have to be resourceful.

Photograph by Norman G Dyhrenfurth

The de-mystifying effect of tourism. Well, you asked – and there it is.
A welcome pause half way up the Namche hill.

Photograph by Lawrence Shian

Trekking in Nepal is an addictive experience and once is seldom enough. The pine forested trail is above the Bhote Kosi close to its confluence with the Dudh Kosi.

Photograph by Hans Höfer

Tibetan trinkets tempt a party of trekkers at Sanesa. Replicas are now made in Kathmandu and Hong Kong.

Photograph by Hans Höfer

Khumbu lodges have attained a good standard of comfort with imaginative menus to service those who trek independent of an agency. Some utilise alternative technologies such as composting and hydro-electric energy.

Photograph by Frances Klatzel

The 1982 tea-shop trekking experience is typified in a modest lodge above Pheriche: a simple sign juxtaposed with stupendous scenery.

Photograph by Lawrence Shlim

The National Park lodge at Lobuche was built in 1980 by New Zealanders to provide accommodation for the exploding number of trekkers.

Photograph by Mal Clarbrough

Tsering Dolma with her first born child, a daughter, portering on a trek in 1969. She and her Sherpa guide husband now have four girls and two boys. The eradication of smallpox, better nutrition and the coming of the Hillary hospital mean Sherpa families grow larger and more healthy.

Photograph by B.Ned Kelly

For a visitor it always comes time to say goodbye. This little boy's hand had been cut open with broken glass and was treated by the Himalayan Rescue Association doctor. They are watched shyly and gratefully by his mother.

Photograph by Dr David R Shlim

Aches, cold and camaraderie are part of the high altitude trekking experience.
Photograph by Hans Höfer

Lobuche is the last stop before climbing to Everest base camp.
Photograph by Hans Höfer

The sacred Gokyo Lake.
Photograph by Hans Höfer

The view from Cho La, a rocky pass between Gokyo and Pheriche, rewards those with perseverance. The glacial moraine of the youngest mountains in the world still feels as though it is on the move.

Photograph by Hans Höfer

The row of stone *chortens* below Lobuche are memorials for climbers killed on the surrounding mountains. This desolate spot marks the end of too many mountaineers' aspirations.

Photograph by Hans Höfer

Tawoche Peak (6,501 metres, 21,330 feet). The smaller peaks that surround the Khumbu giants are often more shapely, and offer tantalising climbing prospects to those who cherish mountains. Unhampered by fame, sponsors and hassle, these are the realms of pure delight for the ambitious alpinist. But sometimes it's enough just to look.

Photograph by John Cleare

Hillary's head Sherpa, Mingma Tsering, Sir Edmund Hillary and his son Peter pause to reminisce near Khumjung. The peaks behind are Kang Taiga and Thamserku, both of which were first climbed by Hillary-led expeditions.

Photograph by Michael Dillon

The physical toughness, sense of humour and genuine sincerity impress all who work with Sherpas. Nima Tenzing has accompanied many climbing expeditions and treks. He bridges the gap between the "old guard" and the new breed of mountain guides

Photograph by Bruce E Jefferies

Filming in the high mountains is often dangerous and difficult and cannot be done without assistance. Kurt Diemberger has relied for years on his friend Pasang, whom he describes as "strong, even at 8,000 metres, and not famous. It felt very good, to be there (Pumori 1989), with such people — and with these mountains."

Photograph by Kurt Diemberger

One of the Sherpa superstars, Pertemba, managing base camp for the 1985 Norwegian Expedition. Pertemba has not only climbed Everest three times, but is considered one of the best *sirdars* and all round mountaineers.

Photograph by Chris Bonington

Moving blocks of ice the size of houses comprise the lower section of the perilous Khumbu Icefall, making it by far the most dangerous part of climbing Everest. A member of the 1971 International Expedition negotiates a crevasse.

Photograph by John Cleare

Using all the paraphernalia of modern mountaineering, huge loads have to be portered across the icefall to support camps higher up on the mountain.

Photograph by John Cleare

Leo Dickinson photographed his own feet, looking down a crevasse in the Khumbu Icefall. One of nature's vices, bottomless crevasses wait to catch the unwary, or the unlucky. One Sherpa fell 55 metres (180 feet) yet somehow survived.

Photograph by Leo Dickinson

Sunset at Camp II at 6,500 metres (21,300 feet) on the southwest face of Everest, on an international expedition led by Col Jimmy Roberts and Norman Dyhrenfurth.

Photograph by John Cleare

The Americans' Camp II in a storm at 6,700 metres (22,000 feet) on the West Ridge of Everest on the north side in 1983.

Photograph by Galen Rowell

Three American climbers are traversing the West Ridge of Everest below the final rock tower at 7,600 metres (25,000 feet), photographed just as the clouds parted. Seeing them so small gives a true sense of scale that sometimes escapes even those climbing.

Photograph by Galen Rowell

An icy blizzard rages around American climbers as they negotiate a corniced ridge, sensationally illustrating the hardships of mountaineering.

Photograph by Galen Rowell

20 April 1985 Pertemba Sherpa (centre) and two Norwegian mountaineers stand on the summit of Everest. The Norwegian Everest Expedition led by Arne Naess broke several Himalayan records. Amongst their achievements were: The largest number of people on the summit from any single expedition (17 reached the top); two successive oldest persons on the summit (Chris Bonington then Dick Bass); first spring expedition to have completed all of its summit bids by 1 May; and Sungdare Sherpa became the first person to have climbed Everest four times.

Photograph by Norwegian Everest Expedition

Evening in the Khumbu. Ama Dablam, Kang Taiga and Thamserku.
Photograph by Peter Hillary

Jet stream winds paint whispy clouds which capture the last rays of the setting sun over Kwangde (6,187 metres, 20,298 feet).

Photograph by Mal Clarbrough

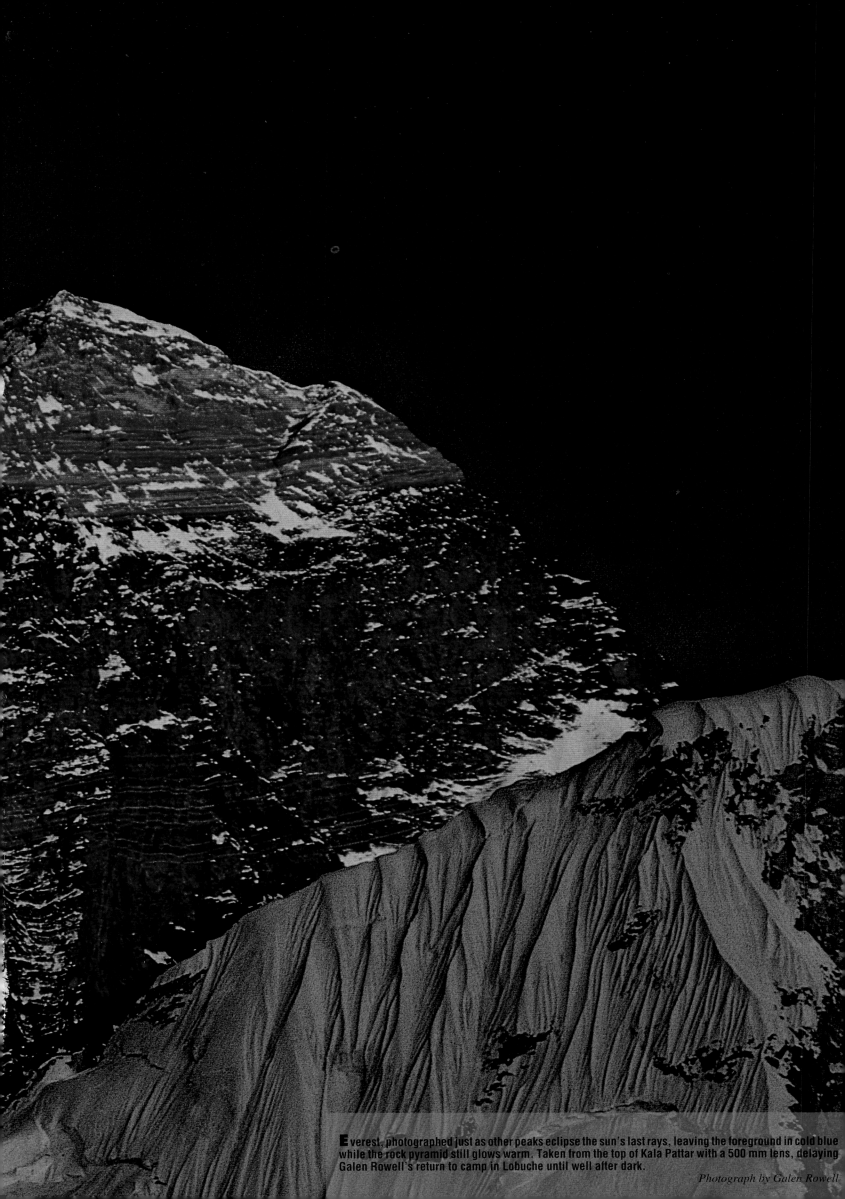

Everest, photographed just as other peaks eclipse the sun's last rays, leaving the foreground in cold blue while the rock pyramid still glows warm. Taken from the top of Kala Pattar with a 500 mm lens, delaying Galen Rowell's return to camp in Lobuche until well after dark.

Photograph by Galen Rowell

Everest before dawn, taken at the very moment that Reinhold Messner and Peter Habeler were making their way to the summit on their historic 1978 climb in which they ascended without using any bottled oxygen, a feat previously considered physiologically impossible. The mountain was too big and the climbers too small for Leo Dickinson to spot them.

Photograph by Leo Dickinson

An extraordinary variety of people with close connections to Everest were invited by Sir Edmund Hillary to contribute to this book. They were asked to give photographs that portray the spirit or capture a special moment in the Khumbu that was personally important to them. Proceeds would go to the Himalayan Trust for, amongst other projects, the reconstruction of the Thyangboche monastery. Their response was magnificent, as evidenced in this book.

Conceived as a fundraising venture by Singapore-based publisher-photographer **Hans Höfer**, the project was orchestrated from Kathmandu by **Lisa Choegyal** with help from Himalayan-expert **Elizabeth Hawley** and editor **Wendy Brewer Lama**. Höfer Press donated the initial production costs and Hans Höfer gave many of his own photographs from Khumbu treks. He also worked on the design and layout of the book with German professor **V.Barl**.

Some background on each contributor enriches the viewers' understanding of the pictures and their historical or cultural significance. Some of the photographers need little introduction, while others are less well-known. With obvious editorial restrictions, the captions do not always fully express the comments of each contributor, although we have tried our best. The photographs, however, span a period of over 30 years and speak for themselves.

Many who were approached Hillary knew personally and some only by name, but all have attachment or affinity with Everest. The result is a remarkable collection of images of Sagarmatha and a unique historical collaboration of Himalayan enthusiasts.

As might be expected of the highest mountain in the world, many of its advocates are mountaineers and climbers. Several donors are amongst the select number of persons who have stood on its summit. **Chris Bonington**, the British climber, photographer and writer, is the best known of these and indeed for a few days even held the record as the oldest person on top. He has organised and led many Himalayan ascents and reached the summit with the 1985 Norwegian Everest Expedition, led by the eclectic Norwegian shipping tycoon **Arne Naess**, husband of singer Diana Ross. **Lord Hunt**, better known as John Hunt, led the historic 1953 ascent and went on to a distinguised public career of youth training activities and political appointments. **Peter Hillary** literally followed in his famous father's footsteps when he climbed Everest by the South Col route in 1990.

Other renowned climbers who have significantly contributed to the history of Himalayan mountaineering include Austrian **Kurt Diemberger**, the only person to have made two first ascents of 8,000-metre mountains, Broad Peak and Dhaulagiri, and **Norman G Dyhrenfurth**, filmmaking son of famous climbing parents, who led the 1963 American Everest Expedition which achieved the first traverse and first ascent of the West Ridge.

John Tyson, a pioneer explorer of the Kanjiroba Himal of west Nepal since 1953, was until recently headmaster of Buddhanilkantha School in Kathmandu and now lives in the Lake District of England. **Hamish MacInnes** took part in Himalayan forays from as early as 1953 and is internationally recognised as a mountain rescue expert, working from his remote home in Glencoe, Scotland.

Mountaineering and wildlife filmmakers are a specialised breed and many of the foremost amongst them are represented here. **Michael Dillon** of Australia has made many documentaries, several about Hillary and the Khumbu. **B Ned Kelly** has prepared many television films including series for David Attenborough and the BBC Natural History Unit and has been visiting his Sherpa friends in the Khumbu since the 1960s.

Dieter and **Mary Plage** worked for several years in Nepal in the 1970s and produced some wildlife classics for Survival Anglia television, including one featuring the fauna in the Everest region.

Long term Nepal residents and naturalists **Robert** and **Linda Fleming** gave many of their superb wildlife shots. Fleming's book, *Birds of Nepal*, remains a standard work on the subject. **Michael Oppitz** is a German anthropologist who worked for many years in Nepal and traced the Sherpas' origins to eastern Tibet. He made a haunting film on shamanism amongst the Magars of northern Nepal.

Acclaimed British writer **Bruce Chatwin** trekked in the Sagarmatha area with his wife Elizabeth in 1983, following his research amongst the Aborigines of Australia for his book, *The Songlines*. Elizabeth Chatwin writes: "He had enough of that geologically ancient land and was longing to go to some young mountains." Chatwin's account of finding yeti footprints appeared in *Esquire* magazine and in his posthumously published *What Are We Doing Here?*

Several contributors enjoyed the opportunity of living and working in the Everest region and these include wildlife conservation specialists who set up the Sagarmatha National Park on behalf of the New Zealand and Nepal governments. **Bruce E Jefferies** lived in Namche in the 1970s and was succeeded by **Mal Clarbrough** in 1980. Following the establishment of the projects, Jefferies worked in Kathmandu as an advisor in the National Parks and Wildlife Conservation Department. **Frances Klatzel** spent years in Thyangboche where she helped create the library and Sherpa cultural centre.

Leo and **Mandy Dickinson** are both adventurers in their own right – Leo is a veteran of Himalayan ballooning and climbing expeditions and is assisted by Mandy who holds British sky diving records. Briton **Richard Crane** has undertaken some outstanding Himalayan feats to raise money for charities, such as running through the Himalaya from Darjeeling in India to Pakistan in 1983 and bicycling through the range from Bangladesh to China.

Bradford Washburn is Honorary Director of the Boston Museum of Sciences and the "Grand Old Man" of much early mountain exploration and photography, accompanied by his intrepid wife Barbara. Their recent achievements include producing the *National Geographic* map of Everest, requiring a unique agreement between the governments of China and Nepal. Photographer **William Thompson,** who among other pictures took all the stunning aerial shots at the beginning of the book, worked with him on this project. Taken from a Lear jet, Thompson's images show us the Everest massif from an angle never before recorded.

Mountain photographers are inevitably also climbers and this applies to **Galen Rowell**, of Mountain Light Photography, California, and **John Cleare** from England, both acknowledged leaders in their fields with many publications and books to their credit.

Lawrence Shlim is an Oregon-based photographer with an unusual eye. His brother **Dr David R Shlim** is Medical Director of the Himalayan Rescue Association, runs a Western-standard clinic in Kathmandu and is an expert in mountaineering medicine and altitude sickness.

Many others were involved whom we were unable to include, for one reason or another. Our thanks go to **Major H P S Ahluwalia, Barry Bishop, Arnold von Bohlen und Halbach, David Breashears, Dr Charles Clarke, Broughton Coburn, Peter Habeler, Toni Hagen, Elizabeth Hawley, Lute Jerstad, Lars Eric Lindblad, Reinhold Messner, Wolfgang Nairz, Robert Redford, Tony Schilling, Ang Rita Sherpa, Daku Sherpa, Joanna Van Gruisen, Stephen Venables, Ambassador Leon J. Weil** and the **Committee for the Reconstruction of the Thyangboche Monastery.**

"**P**lease support my work through The Himalayan Trust by contributing funds to help with the rebuilding of the Thyangboche monastery and assist the Trust's on-going activities. Please donate US$150 or more and receive a special presentation copy of 'Sagarmartha' sined by myself as personal thank you for your help. Please send your donation today and receive my book to treasure."

Sir Edmund Hillary

Please photocopy this form and return it with your donation of US$150 or more if you wish to receive a special copy of Sagarmatha. Your donation should be send (by crossed cheque made payable to The Himalayan Trust) direct by registered mail to The Himalayan Trust c/o Sir Edmund Hillary, 278A Remuera Road, Auckland 5, New Zealand. Funds can also be directly transferred to The Himalayan Trust Board, account number 0031716-00, Remuera Branch, Bank of New Zealand, Auckland, New Zealand. Please indicate "Sagarmatha Book Donation" with your contribution.

Yes, here is my donation to **The Himalayan Trust**

for US$ _____

(or equal currency)

Please send this book to me★/as my present to★

Name: _____

Address : _____

_____

_____

Name : _____

_____

Signature : _____   Date: _____

•Please delete where necessary